Day

David

Day Return

M.C. Wood

[signature]

Richard Wood

Brimstone Press

First Published in 2007
by Brimstone Press
PO Box 114
Shaftesbury
SP7 8XN

Author contact:
mcwood@brimstonepress.co.uk

Designed and typeset in Times by
Linda Reed and Associates
Shaftesbury
SP7 8NE

Printed by Antony Rowe Ltd
Chippenham
SN14 6LH

First edition of 400 copies

ISBN 978-0-9548171-5-2

Night Thought

I lie alone, in love
In a room that no-one enters but myself,
Outside, in the world, I see the trees wave
In the sky in the rain, filled with their own life.

Kathleen Raine

Contents

Muse

I will dream you a poem,
an anthology leaping;
I'll enter your sleeping
with day-dreams, and blow
until sonnets are spinning
with gold inspiration
and ballads are bouncing
on broken rhymes running
to trochees sent tumbling
to true innovation.

You'll be filled with sestinas,
with rondeaux, sprung rhythm,
so I'll dream you a day
to do nothing at all
but to play with ideas
and to read other poets,
just to scribble and ponder,
to meander and wonder.

Before you are woken
by screeching alarm-clocks,
I will boot up computers
and tap-dance on keys;
you will rise, so be ready –
no coffee, no breakfast –
to find what *you*'ve written
with consummate ease.

Feeble Excuses

Eve: It wasn't my fault, Lord.
You know how it is:
Adam is always hungry and he's very fussy.
He gets fed up with mangoes and bananas…
And he looked up at me,
with those great eyes of his,
crying for *something different*.
So when that silly worm offered me apples,
I thought what a happy choice.

What's this I'm wearing?
Just a little something I ran up
from a couple of fig-leaves.
Don't you think it suits me?

Adam: It wasn't my fault, Lord.
I didn't want another row with Eve at lunch-time.
You know how it is, Lord:
Eat up your oranges and currants.
(If you don't mind me asking, Lord,
could you make spuds less tasty?
Eve says I'm getting fatter by the minute.)
So, when she offers me that apple, what's a guy to do?
Have warfare? In Eden?

Serpent: It wasn't my fault, O Creator of all…
I didn't think.   Remember, Lord,
I haven't had a bite of that darned apple yet.
I easily forget all your instructions.
How is a humble snake to take them in?
(Especially with all that din that humans make,
singing as they prance about.
I have enormous problems
sliding away from their great feet,
to save myself
from being squashed by their dancing.)
I thought I'd give them both a treat.

And really, Lord, Magnificent and Mighty,
what is so wrong that Eve's dressed in a nightie
made out of fig-leaves?

I think it's rather fetching.

Hang-Glider

floats in the wind's path, over a dolphin's trail,
goes dancing to rhythms of waves' liberty,
possesses all, in ear-throbbing trance,
never acknowledging soil-magnets;
eyes scan horizon to ocean below,
ocean to horizon; sea-gull echo,
only an echo, carries the rider;
he will find man-knots soon
when wind-ties
loosen.

The Inevitability of Plugs

Shining bung, dangled innocently
by silver-ball chain, reflects my face
distorted on mirrored surface;
now it holds back basin-water,
yet, one slip, and it becomes
the gateway to Hades, sewers.

We are subject to its vagaries:
a perished rubber seal allows
our water to seep quietly away,
or a gripping-too-tight of the plug-hole,
as a tap   drips,
leads to a flooded bathroom floor.

Telephoto Lens
Inspired by Billy Collins

Old men and rucksacks lean against the stones,
aged themselves as craggy rocks below;
below the rocks, stones as old craggy men,
lean against themselves and aged rucksacks.

Sun shines on sandwiches long dried;
a shadow sheep comes closer, sheltering wind;
a long wind-dried sheep shines, comes
sheltering closer, shadow on sun sandwiches.

Gazing towards them, I see only grey
and yet I know they are on the hills;
yet I, gazing on, and toward grey hills,
see them, know only that they *are*.

Gazing below, I see them, men themselves;
I long know craggy hills, old sandwiches,
that, closer towards, the sun shines,
comes on aged rucksacks,
and that, yet only a shadow, they lean.

Remains

The garage has moved
the notice says
as it flaps in the draught
from the broken pane;

so it has upped
and left behind
old tyres and oil,
tears on the concrete.

Day Return
In memory of John Payne

Bypassing the bird-mark on the pane,
my raindrop races ahead of the others,
takes the shortest route to the sill,
does not appear to waver or be blown
sideways by wind or locomotion;

this is a journey I could do without;
although I've fought boredom, marked
time with bets and private spying games,
and munched raw carrots rather than
buffet meals, I have no wish to arrive;

saying goodbye to someone's never easy;
even if words that baldly tell the truth
remain unsaid, there's still the knowing
that signals from eye to eye and states
as clearly as moving lips;

the train judders, bang-clangs to a halt;
I grab my coat and dawdle to the exit,
willing the platform to extend itself,
to stretch without end, but it has gone.
I take the short path to the hospital.

Here is Sunshine

captured within a sphere; it sits
comfortably in your hand; bear
its full weight: lighter than stone,
heavier than a tennis ball;

nail-scrape its surface; we
are sprayed with Summer;
dig deeper; soft suede pith
gloves half-moon segments

clinging together,
forming an inner mass,
compacted droplets, juice
encased in finest satin;

try a segment; eat; remember Nice?
Your chair parked under an orange tree?
Remember the fragrance?
Remember crisp rustling?

Watch out;
the seeds inside are little pips,
bitter as bile, or as Winter.

Fitting In

One night, she found herself inside
a shoe-box and she couldn't fit;
her legs and arms stuck out,
her mouth was cardboard gagged
and when she moved, the sides
came closer, squeezing her.

All night, she tried to mould
herself into a block, no luck;
she thought of jettisoning her mind,
biting her arms and legs to stumps;
she couldn't reach.
The walls caved in.

Her boy-friend called –
a jolt upright to breakfast smells,
computer screens, deadlines to meet,
leaving her other life behind
in fields and gardens, books,
scraps – half-written poetry.

Instructions

She told him
what to wear and what to do;
she told him
who to see and how to grow
his hair, and when to buy
another car.

He told her
where to go.

Old Bridge just outside Budapest

This is a place to which I must return
        however far I travel;
these arches entice me, my eyes are held
        by their mêlée of colour.

Maybe I have never fully absorbed
        the content of the stalls,
nor do I always remember which
        arch held which shop,

yet I'm drawn to the undulation,
        perfect lines of brickwork,
despite the detail
        that I cannot always recall.

Before Sleep

From the overgrown vine,
        blue fruit drip,
strange amongst rose-bushes,
        self-seeded,
perhaps, but we ate only
        red tomatoes.

Slice through skin,
        dry parchment,
a cascade of nectar,
        fluorescent,
bursts upon the kitchen
        and the scent,

the scent, pungent, spicy,
        seeps into every pore.

Passport Photo

Don't press the button 'til you're ready.

Walls conceal mildewed memories:
plans for foreign holidays behind
pale nylon curtains, import/export files
tarnishing oblong mirrors;   I perch,
uncomfortably, on the wobbly stool,
grimacing at lights.

Don't press the button...
but I will never be ready.

A strange face confronts, mimicking;
its glasses glint spitefully.
I will never
be ready to leave this kiosk,
to wait
with all the supermarket eyes upon me
until that gargoyle, sticky new-born,
in triplicate, dives from the slot,
ready to haunt me for a decade.

Boy with Lights

Boy on a pogo-stick,
bouncing in flashing red
thrown from the sign
above the barber's shop;
boy bouncing green, white,
green, white,
on wet pavements
under Christmas trees
along the High Street;
boy flickering
red, yellow, green
by the nightclub.

Boy alone,
dark, a black jack-in-a-box,
making for home,
a small torch lifting, falling
urgently,   heading
for where he may be seen
with tee-shirt and jeans
on two feet.

Come Buy

Three-bed-roomed fake –
the residents have tried
with Dulux paints to imitate
the feel of real Georgian.
The patio, that's also fake
and paved, they call a terrace,
consisting mostly of a pond,
water-lilies and goldfish;
these are included in the selling price.
Roses and clematis mask garden walls,
which, and we take no responsibility
for this statement, *buyer beware* and all that,
seem intact.

Viewers of this property
are advised to   tip   toe
around the outside of the building;
chaffinches nest in the arch by the garage
and house martins build above the window
of the en suite bathroom;
                    mind your head;
droppings may be easily wiped
from paintwork with a damp rag.
The smallest bedroom doubles at present
as a study for a sometime poet, and boasts,
for her efforts, an ample fitted cupboard;
this could easily be adapted into a wardrobe.
Interested purchasers may wish to update
the delightfully old-fashioned three-year-old kitchen.

Structurally sound, this property is light
and might suit an eccentric elderly couple
who are unconcerned by the lack
of entertainment and pizzazz
of the meadow area of the market town
near which this building stands;
see reference: www.drahus.BL@loco/props.co.uk.

Underground Refugees

Lost in transit
at the end of the line?
In a box kept for people
who are mislaid on the railway
or one put aside for those
who are at their wits' end?

Opera 1939–1945

When my father went to war,
my mother sang *One Fine Day*
in a soft contralto from dawn to dusk
until we children knew it all by heart
and sang along; somehow we knew
the Pinkerton she sought was not
our Dad, the setting some romantic dream
in which she played the heroine;
she was a Madam Butterfly
washing dishes in suburbia,
living handy for the shops,
with two small boys, and baby Jill,
who cried, and Gran who limped,
a garden filled with flowering shrubs
and one contented cat, but she
would never glance at these, nor,
when our Dad returned, at him.
She just stopped singing.

Welcome

Your house is ice; the atmosphere
tones with the décor, cream and white;
your tone, *Delighted that you came, my dears,*
splinters the smile you squeeze, so bright,

so carefully arranged, in keeping with
your seating, stunningly achieved
so that there is an air about you
banning comfort from your doorway.

We remove our shoes.

Party Politics

Cocktails and canapés... Waiters pass
between the black-tied and the bare-shouldered
swerving silently, skaters in slow motion.

Under chandeliers' gleam, a ring of light,
a tall woman, a small man; he bends,
takes a slither of celery; she raises an arm.

She churns the air; he lifts his arms
across his chest as she comes closer;
he gnashes one green stick after another.

One of her feet brushes his shoe;
he lifts his right arm; his eyes close;
hands on hips, she moves forward.

He sips his empty glass, grabs
a carrot baton, swallows it whole;
well above his head, she beats her chest.

He steps backwards; she follows.

Gong. Stillness. He slips into the mêlée.
She stares at the empty crudités bowl.

Miss Match

You are an indoor girl married
                              to an outdoor man
who dreams of spaces,
                              fills his mind with trees
and longs for roses, honeysuckle,
                              bluebells, pinks and lilies.

You dream of clothes and films,
                              of dances and romance;
he brings you bunches of fine
                              carrots, leeks and cabbages
fit for a princess, and would bring you
                              children, but you turn away.

You drift from room to room in satin slippers
                              skirting clods
that he's brought in from digging, and you
                              lay his place
with silver cutlery, little napkins
                              and china fine as wafers.

He eats nouvelle cuisine and sips his Shiraz,
                              thanks you, smiles,
leaves for the garden, digs
                              a deeper wider trench
and plants digitalis, a yew tree
                              and a golden laburnum.

The Pied Piper of Aberfan

No gaudy piper led them
on this ordinary Welsh Friday
to this ordinary Welsh school
but all the little children,
bright-faced and eager,
gathered just the same.

There was no rush
to settle at their desks,
the only music chair-scrape
and happy chat –

Did you see Mam's new dress?
Willy's football hit the line,
blackened the washing –

until the teachers hushed each class
and the song was bees on gilly-flowers,

until it changed to a rumbling,
groans, as the earth slid back
to where it wished to be,
away from the hillside.

Our homes are silent now
in Aberfan and Merthyr;
no music draws our children
from school, nor from the spoil.

Small Café in Josefov
Prague, Czech Republic

The Jewish Quarter –
but, exploring museums and synagogue,
there are few Jews.

For us, the need is somewhere
out of the sun, cool,
dark, away from the crush.

What is this place?
We sit under a replica gibbet
in a room filled with framed documents.

*Someone left these papers
and that battered briefcase,
that single shoe…*

Waiters emerge from darkness,
bustle, smiling, around us,
bring us coffee and snacks.

*Some places reach out
until they are huge;
others are eaten away.*

*This is a place that's shrunk,
leaving this building ,*

somehow, in limbo…

Some of us, rooted
firmly in one place,
sit where our parents sat.

The dis-ease of here
makes bitter biscuits.
We don't stay long.

Emigrée

Nothing of her exterior betrays
the hole beneath her skin; she wears
smart clothes; her make-up glows with health;
a careful smile, eyes' shine, voice low
present the person that we almost know.

Sometimes, she seems absorbed in fantasy
and clings to those she almost knows
until we feel strangled, though we comprehend
her incompleteness; like a phantom limb,
the space she bears is smarting.

We meet her in town, at weddings;
she's a friend of friends; her English is perfect.
Her background? Maybe Czech or Polish
or Irish, even Canadian. She lives here,
but incompletely. There is a fissure in her soul.

Knowing Where to Start

Let me introduce you to this poem;
it began in nonsense, then stole feathers
from dreams, so that, suddenly,
I became a bird; you will hear
my chirp, and I hope that you
understand that I sing Freedom.
Can you feel how these word-wings
soar, carry me upwards to meaning,
release thoughts from earth-bindings,
allow discovery, as I glide
over new territory?

Let me take you with me.
Grab a word or two to spring from.
Here we go.

Poets in the Supermarket

It's open, the museum for lost souls,
who wander laden avenues and gaze
morning-eyed blankly, as they slow-patrol
starred special exhibits, *Today's Reduced Prices.*
It's an eight a.m. shock to the system,
Monday's quest for dog-food cans.

Experienced sexogenarians trolley-clash,
trawling for bargains in the fruit and veg;
non-cooks gaze hungrily at instant mash,
canned soup, dark chocolate and fudge;
at tills, pale ghosts, ready to write a poem,
pack overheard phrases, bear them home.

Never Being

Before they had really learned to love,
an idea's seed dropped roots and stealthily
took form, and they became enchanted by
its presence, its shape became, in their eyes,
flawless, its unfelt movements strong and healthy;
they imagined holding it in their arms, watching
it play happily at their feet, and, above all, they
dreamed of its smile and its dependence on them.
They fed this non-child with all their attention
so that it became perfect, all they could wish for;
it grew tall and all was well, until it asked to be born,
and each of the non-parents wanted it too much.
When it had no life, they tugged at the idea, split
the phantom child, and tore themselves apart.

Bread-Making

Such preparation before I start:
sifting of strong flour to talcum mist,
finger-tip feeling of water – is this tepid?

Inside my head, ingredients gather:
hurt for words unsaid, deeds undone;
resentment festers, muscles tighten.

Concentrate on well-making, a place
to rest magic putty, sprinkle sugar,
flood my mixture.

I'm holding back, gripping
a chair, a table, steadying myself,
mouth taut, unwilling to spill word-lava.

Now I must guard the cauldron,
this cool-spitting geyser
that transforms pale mud to dough.

If he were here, nothing would contain
my volcano, the full force scorching
every word he uses to placate me.

But now, the joy of it, sleeves rolled
above elbows, body curved over table;
I raise rubbery softness, thump to pastry board;

raise, thump, a heavy engine's piston.
Dough moulds to my hands.
Muscles tense and relax,

until dough feels like silk,
ready to be stretched and eased
to be left for first proving,

waiting

to take all my shoulder-strength
thumping and raising, before
easing, shaping anger

and baking a crisp light loaf.

Coup de Grâce

They shot the writer
but his words keep spilling out
into the future.

A Day for Rest

There's something curious about the way
God formed the years and months and weeks.
Perhaps He was too busy with his Waters
and His considering of what to put under them,
or did the Heavens fill His mind with stars
                              and meteors?
Was He absorbed with the firework display
                    of volcanic eruptions,
or exactly how to harness solar energy?

Reaching the end of His deliberations,
planning an autonomous wilful being,
He had thought of Man.
He must have been exhausted.

Therefore,
it is hardly surprising that He dreamed
the Seventh Day – A Day for Rest –
but then He seemed to spread it about the week,
leaving Mankind to choose
which day to worship Him
              and so, as far as I can gather,
Moslems chose Fridays, Jews took Saturdays,
Christians Sundays, and probably someone
has Mondays to Thursdays.

It becomes impossible to organise a World-Wide Lie-In.

Chrome Summer

Extreme heat – we rest
in umbrella-shade in the garden;
even through drowsy lids,
our eyes are bathed
in a dazzle of sun-flowers,
and we dream colour:
fieldfuls of dandelions,
the first touch of Autumn,
beech leaves twisting out of green.
We dream sunlight on puddles,
cycling to school in smog,
dense to the nostrils.
I see pus, as my grandfather
lances a boil...
                    and our child's face,
jaundiced on hospital pillows,
a single light in the village at midnight
and a bright toy lorry left on a rug
                    to be tripped over
after a long day.

Struggling

Water heaves violently;
lilies are thrust
into seething tangles at the pond's edge;
grass-snake's coils flash;
as they thrash,
a hard v-mouth grasps
something, a frog, pink
with struggling to release
frail water-dancer's toes;
fish hang in rows, watch
hypnotised, until
the frog jerks
and escapes.

The room heaves; chairs
go flying to all sides
as *he* performs strange
animal leaps into spaces
between diners, who
pretend not to be seeing
the boy, who says
learned phrases only
and can't feel their wanting
to communicate, nor
their inability to cope
with his difference
and their need
to escape.

The room heaves, lilies
go flying to all sides,
as *he* thrashes a tangle
of strange spaces
between a grass-snake,
who pretends not to be seeing,
between fish, who struggle,
wanting to communicate,
hypnotised by their
inability to cope, and
a hard pink frog, who says
This boy is different,
and hides from him
behind a chair.

Smile Please

These days, even DNA poses
for the camera, dancing
across pages of Sunday supplements;
unimagined colour-flashes catch
our eyes; tendrils of cells,
magnified to exotic blooms,
sway in blood rivers, captivate.

We are led into fantasy, far
from the gore of operating theatres,
battlefields, road-accidents;
we delight in corpuscles,
are charmed by pores;
blood is a diversion; let's see more.

The Sacrifice of Laocoon *(sic: and his sons)*
Fresco by Guido Romano, Ducal Palace, Milan

What bad luck
that Laocoon was born a Trojan
and that Apollo preferred Greeks.
Typical of the god,
he didn't dirty his hands,
but hired two serpents,
mighty bully-boys,
to crush the priest.

Of course,
serpents are not content
with one assassination;
wholesale slaughter's more their line,
and in this painting,
which could have been a scoop
for a freelance photographer,
Laocoon almost misses his fate.

One son is just about kneeling,
balanced on one leg only;
the other falters;
we can almost feel him
swaying, flailing, tumbling senseless,
as Laocoon, half-dressed, brandishing his club,
comes thundering into the picture.

Naturally, if you look away from the turmoil,
you'll see Apollo watching on a distant cloud.

Ghazal for Bête Noire

Perhaps it would be possible to mine your shell,
uncovering your identity, hiding there: perhaps

taking a tour of your intestinal tract, determining
your taste in food, and what you drink, perhaps;

perhaps, within the confines of your face, I'd understand
what makes you laugh, what makes you cry; perhaps

I'd surf your veins, your arteries, discover flow
of energy into your movements, then, perhaps,

red-water raft a route towards your feet
discovering the paths you trod; perhaps,

squeezing myself inside the tiniest of cells,
I'd trek through labyrinthine secrets in your genes; perhaps

your mind might tell me what your motives are
and, in your body, I might empathise with you. Perhaps.

Reunion

This hotel lobby drips worn gilt and chandeliers;
memories of Nazi headquarters lurk in corners.

I recognise her immediately: her height, her red hair,
although her shoulders bear the weight of otherness.

Aware of slick waiters who survey her clothes,
she's awkward, but we greet each other fondly.

Come to my home for tea, she says, gesturing
at swing doors, polished glass and brass.

Do I detect a foreign click?
A hint of Czech about her English?

Is she as I'd imagined? She half fits this place
and half the place she's left behind;

outside, grey drizzle, unspoken questions.

Tunnel to the Car Park

There is no visible O of light ahead,
as we plunge into walkway twists;
as we grope walls, our feet crunch
on glass shards and tangle with sprigs
of wire, and we curse some youth
for whom beating-up lighting
was yesterday's high;
nor is there light behind us now
where lamp-lit night has given way
to tar-moist black; no smell of diesel
lingers here, only urinals' stench
and a whiff of something
vaguely familiar, unpleasant.
We move faster.
Are those feet ours
splashing, tapping, echoing?

At last, tunnel walls emerge,
glowing graffiti, catching
fluorescent lights from signs
of the shopping centre.
We stride on,
drumming hearts slowing,
flashing keys to safety.

Short Journey through the Sahara

Away from all that is familiar,
over the moonscape, ochre dunes,
we sway, on uncomfortable rough-
backed beasts, and sky and sand-hills
are all we see, and all we feel is
lashing of the rough wind's tongue
and the cold on our faces.

In misted distance, palms. An oasis?
No, sun-on-sand shimmering,
an illusion of water.
No water here, just sun, shining,
drying, so that exposed skin
sheds grit-sheets and we become
particles of the desert.

A short journey, this, but one
touching infinity, feeling
the universe, as camels and riders
lurch through possibilities.

On the Tube

What must the other passengers have thought?
Or was I the only one who saw
the pigeon flutter through the open door
at the last station? Weren't they taught
to look?

Well out of place, but still at home, content,
it pecked precisely at the long-barred carriage floor.
Nature and Man's graffiti never
meant to meet in there – and to be seen, if only
by my eyes.

So many years ago, I really can't recall,
five of us took a trip to Drury Lane...
four boys and I... the tube train home again.
Downing the escalator to the booking hall,
one bulging pocket...

I took it back, facing cold stares and travellers' smiles,
fluttering captive carefully held within one hand.
Feathers-trail-telling pigeon and flushed man
traversed the downward movement upward miles
to light.

Fetching the Sunday Papers

No-one walks through the market-place
at this hour, on a day like this.
From the last storm, water has gathered
in roadside runnels, and dust has turned
to mud, and floating nests of debris

swirl towards blocked drains,
which no-one clears until tomorrow.
Rain-soaked brick gleams in a moment of sun,
yet no birdsong accompanies my footsteps,
over pavements, where poets' verses glint.

Wall-eyed mannequins stare
through spattered shop windows;
a road-sign catches sodden pages
that the storm has blown; yesterday's news,
outside-our-town's gossip, wars,

politics and crime hang, drooping bunting.
Clouds rise; raindrops dance polka-dots by my boots;
I splash homeward, bearing proof
that people exist, everywhere,
even on a day like this.

Unwanted Silences
In the Kitchen

Unexpectedly freed, the cat
wanders the flower-filled house,
sleeps on forbidden pillows, gnaws
and sucks sheets, scratches
nests on cushions;
only the kitchen door is shut;
some-one has removed lists
from the pear fridge-magnet,
and empty carriers lie folded
on the table by till receipts;
some-one has buffed the tiles,
so that yesterday's prints
have disappeared and surfaces
gleam like mirrors, too bright
for the silent house;
too tidy too are regimented trays
of dainty snacks, awaiting guests
who are not hungry.

Arousal

At night, earth shifts;
minute fissures expose green tips,
so that the morning ritual,
drawing of blinds,
displays newness.

Everything pushes silently,
moss-stealing over stones.
Lately, I've felt a murmur in my hands,
caught stirrings in my ears,
heard feet rustling.

Trees swell;
look at the hazel-dangle, pollen cloudy;
a wagtail struts the pavement by the pub;
moorhens and ducks flotilla on the Stour.
We become ant hills of restlessness;

fingers twitch;
toes, accustomed to resting,
demand to walk;
eyes, weary of screens and paper,
walls and windows, mark every change.

Listen, the wren calls:
Sap, sap, sap: the sap is rising.

Early Monday

All down the valley between duvet mounds
and mattress, your breathing sighs, a strong pulse
of you, caught by poly-cotton waves, bound

feetwards; my side of the bed is still; vigilance
is motionless, as I lie, as I wait for dawn.
Beside me, you struggle, caught in a sleep-web.

You thrash against invisible binding threads.
As you become more entwined, the heat
you generate becomes intensified; you tug,

you heave, and the duvet finally leaves my side.
In the dim room, I shiver, naked; I slide
to the floor, smother cold flesh in dressing-gown

and draw curtains; light quells your storm.
You lie still, floating on calm sheets.

After the Caring Years

A sudden swirl – and it's as if
water's breached my defences,
crumbled years building walls
to keep my son safe,
and to imprison me,
not knowing how to walk free,
though doors were opening,
not knowing how to greet a world
where I was almost a stranger.

Now this world comes to me,
greets an uncertain stranger,
who can't converse, has no gossip,
save on new medical discoveries,
who has forgotten how to travel,
except by ambulance.

I find myself floating,
catching breath with excitement,
alive again.

Night Walk
Terza Rima

Only the snap
of twigs and the path's feel
illuminate my mind's-eye map.

Clouds part, showing enough steel
moonlight to reveal neat
images, flat, ready to peel,

monochrome, from the sheet
in a child's *Horror Book of Things
Under the Bed,*

recalled nightmares, ghouls that spring
out of slippers. *Keep on track,*
I tell myself. *Perhaps sing*

to frighten shadows from my back?
One moves beside me, but pale light
displays a gorse-bush, ready to attack

unwary passers-by; my fears take flight;
I speed homewards through a friendly night.

The Good Thing
In response to John Wain's The Bad Thing

Often just being alone seems the good thing.
Solitude slips into my working life,
filling my mind with calm, with recollections
of past activities, and ideas for exploring,
a silent triumph over everyday rush and clatter.
It is timeless, this good thing. It is now; it was then,
but it is fragile. The post, a neighbour's call,
and solitude's broken; you are left clinging to fragments.

Then, you think, this good thing is nascent in you.
Just being alone is not required for solitude;
not peace, nor happiness, nor escaping into dreams
is necessary. Don't weep at its loss. Undamaged
by interruptions, it's merely carefully wrapped,
tucked away, handy to reach. Grasp it now.

Birth Day

You did not play football
against the goal-posts of my ribs,
nor did you swim so fast
in the wash of my uterus
that every meal I took
leapt to my throat;
        no, love,
that was your brother's way,
        but you
silently announced that you intended
to be born then, not in the month
charted by nurses, doctors, your parents.
Even in embryo you showed your strength.
I felt your presence before even a twinge
of back-ache, before even a drop of moisture.
Your slide-shute arrival was no surprise,
nor was the month you chose to be born in,
April, Spring and sudden storm.

Neon-Lit by Lanterns

At night, the road is a set
for a film shot in tones of sepia
and, on rainy evenings,
the slates become bronze.

As I leave the house,
the terrace opposite blinks
through a drizzle net-curtain;
there ought to be music,

an overture for a story of intrigue,
set in the Georgian era,
for our houses look Georgian,
but they are no more Georgian

than they are a film set,
and there will be no music
save for the steady drip
from over-filled gutters,

distant town's traffic hum,
creaks of the pine tree
by the road's entrance
and the swish
of my wellingtons in the puddles.

Yang Lian and the Photo of Durdle Door

You note rock strata, build
strata of coloured words,
evoking a time, a place,
a presence.
Photo-waves fly on copper rays.
I would like to be there, you say,
*but today ends; only this view
is possible.* Flight so early
reveals only blank paper of cloud
awaiting imagination.
You are silent; are you listening
to the strum of birds' wings by cliffs
that leap from wall to eyes
ready to receive camera-memory?

Or are you by another ocean, that
has wave-worn anger into new poetry,
that has tide-washed memories
into clarity of thought, cleansed
red savagery of massacre to a dream
of sunset on cliffs, used stone,
that silenced voices, to rebuild time?

You turn, review Now,
answer questions,
the effects of trauma on a poet.
Voices in translation show
how your mind's chisel
fashions hope from chaos.

Expenditure
Villanelle

There's no-one can recapture time that's spent;
memories become vague outlines of the past
and photographs deceive as we grow old.

Whilst we can recollect and reinvent,
the truth explodes, hide from the blast:
'There's no-one can recapture time that's spent.'

Though we wrote diaries everywhere we went,
aiming to catch details, life's too fast
and photographs deceive as we grow old.

Try as we will, we still cannot prevent
years slipping by, shed like beech mast.
There's no-one can recapture time that's spent.

You say, my years stay back to some extent.
Such blatant flattery leaves me quite aghast
and photographs deceive as we grow old.

As years slip by, I am content,
provided the outlook's not too overcast.
There's no-one can recapture time that's spent
and photographs deceive as we grow old.

Acknowledgements

My thanks:

to the editors of *The West in her Eye*,
Tears in the Fence, *Darius Poetry Anthology*,
Dorset Perspectives and other ESP publications
in which some of these poems have originally
appeared in various forms;

to *Beehive Press* and the organisers
of *The London Drama Writing Challenge
1996/1997* for encouraging my first public readings;

to Pam Zimmerman-Hope & Zenobia Venner
and all the Poets of Poetry Dorchester;

to all the East Street Poets;

to Paul Hyland and his 2006 Dorchester Poets;

and, above all, to Richard, without whose
encouragement I would never have produced
this book.

M.C.Wood   April 2007